Conversations with the Heart

Janae Werdlow

Copyright © 2014. Janae Werdlow

All rights reserved. This book or any portion thereof may not be reproduced or used in any manner whatsoever without the express written permission of the publisher except for the use of brief quotations in a book review or scholarly journal.

ISBN: 978-0-692-33765-3

Dedicated to the love of my life, my muse, whoever he may be

"Expose yourself to your deepest fear; after that, fear has no power, and the fear of freedom shrinks and vanishes. You are free."

– Jim Morrison

Preface

Often times we speak kindly and encourage others while forgetting to do the same for ourselves. I want this book to remind you of the pieces of yourselves we try too often to forget. Your heart is an essential part to life, anatomically as it is figuratively. Treat it well and have conversations with it as often as you can. You will find yourself having more inner peace that way. I hope this book sparks some conversations with your friends, with potential loves and most importantly with God and yourself.

Dear Heart,

Hey!

We have to talk.

It's been a long time since I've acknowledged you and I'm sorry.

I thought if I used you less, I wouldn't hurt anymore

I thought if I forgot you, you'd go away.

But I need you to live... To love.

You're still there,

Even though I'm scared to fall.

In the back of my mind I still want to

To love. Some day.

Dear Heart,
You give of yourself too freely.
You don't have a proper valuation of yourself.
You are beautiful,
You are powerful,
You are God's gift to the world.
There's nothing wrong with proclaiming that
If it were not so, you would not have been born
Children are **gifts** from God.
That does not change because you have grown up.
You are validated
By me
By God
You don't need it from anyone else.

Dear Heart,

Nothing beautiful **asks** for attention

It is given

You

Are

Beautiful

And I will honor your beauty

By waiting

Waiting to be seen

Waiting to be cherished

Waiting to be loved

Because you are entirely too beautiful to BEG for

attention

Dear Heart,
Why won't you listen?
One message whispered and yet somehow you misunderstood.
No telephone.
Obviously, my head is the thinker here.
It has the brains.
You're just a dreamer.
My mind said, "no."
My mind said, "Don't listen."
My mind said, "It's not worth it."
But here you are making feelings AGAIN.
I can't live like this.
Emotional hopscotch is no fun to play.
Don't put me in the game unless you know for sure the guy is in the same!
I don't like it when I go all around the board, just to go back to jail again.

Dear Heart,

We are finally on the same page.

You loving life and me with no problems.

We're almost friends again.

It hasn't been like this since I was a kid.

What changed?

I liked it better when the sandbox had castles instead of cooties.

I liked it better when he would unfreeze me in tag,

Versus after school fondling.

No more red rovers of men coming over with no tell signs of if they actually want to come over or lay over me.

Life didn't used to be this complicated.

Thanks for staying by me.

Dear Heart,

We're better off alone.

Don't mistake disrespect for false affection.

Don't settle for not acting right, thinking it'll get right.

Demand someone worth your time.

Be worth the effort and don't settle for less!

The lesser brings pain and unnecessary drama. Trust me when I say we're better off alone.

We're better off alone.

Dear Heart,

I know I take you through a lot.

I know I place the blame on you too much,

When most of our problems are because of me.

But I'm thankful for you.

Thanks.

Just in case, I don't say it enough.

Dear Heart,

Does it hurt?

When I have a scar, I pick at it.

Even though I know it'll hurt just because I hate looking at the scab.

I make it bleed all over again because I have no self-control.

I think that's what I'm doing to you.

I don't mean to.

I just have no self-control.

I throw you into situations over and over again thinking it'll be different,

But they're not.

Situations change, but the guys stay the same.

I have to stop doing that to you ...

But I don't know any better,

I was taught fairy tales in love lessons.

Dear Heart,

I hear some music down there.

Is there a party going on?

A celebration?

It's official.

He loves me.

All the times he *loved me not,* will be worth it now,

I promise.

Just you wait.

Dear Heart,

Do you know what the word grieve means?

Probably not.

You're an anatomical organ; you don't know what a dictionary is.

It basically means somebody that we loved left.

They're no longer with us.

All we have are memories.

And it's going to hurt like hell ...

For a long time.

It's similar to heartbreak and we've dealt with that before.

You're stronger than you think.

This also doesn't have a cure.

Only time slipping by will dull the pain.

Only sunshine and plenty of it, dries the rain.

Dear Heart,

Cut it out!

I am putting my foot down.

You will not like this man.

You will not have feelings for him.

You will not.

I specifically said no!

...

Why don't you ever listen to me?

Fine!

You win

This time.

And if this goes wrong...

It'll be **your** fault!

Dear Heart,

What's all that racket down there?!

Are you......

BUILDING????

Well I... I didn't even know you knew how to build.

So what are you building?

are you trying to have a new landscape?

Is it a sculpture?

Maybe a feng shui garden?

Oh,

A wall.

Correction: Walls.

Well that's not very aesthetically pleasing.

What are you building walls for?

They're too high.

You won't be able to see a thing.

And they're so thick.

You won't hear when someone is knocking and there's no door!

You won't be able to let anyone in.

You won't be able to get out.

Oh.

Well I see.

That's the point,

isn't it?

Dear Heart,

There is a war being waged.
I can feel the cuts of words yelled.
The deep bruises of past baggage,
The scars left from battles where no one wins.
I don't expect you to take off your armor,
Hold tight to your shield.
The victor is coming.
He eventually will be unveiled.
Until then don't give up,
Don't throw your faith to fate.
I promise prince charming is coming
Just wait

Dear Heart,

I'm being fearless today.

I will love without regard for how badly I may be hurt.

I will freely give the love I have to share.

I will not regard the past for my future.

We will fly on the wings of love today,

Fly with me

Dear Heart,
I know it's tempting to think it's your fault,
But I want you to know that <u>they</u> <u>walked</u> <u>away</u>.
They did!
You can't nitpick at yourself thinking you weren't good enough for them to stay.
It's natural to want to blame yourself,
All you can see are your mistakes,
But that isn't why they left.
They left because they weren't strong enough,
Man enough,
Woman enough,
To accept all of you.
Love is
UNCONDITIONAL.
It doesn't identify only with strengths,
It accepts AND fortifies weakness.
It does not walk away.
It does not fail.

You didn't make anyone leave,
You simply gave them the liberty to leave,
Be thankful they did.

Dear Heart,

How others see you, is not important.

How you see yourself means everything.

Who are you?

If you don't know, neither do I.

The moment you feel like you have to prove your worth to someone is the moment you need to walk away from them.

Don't be afraid to rock the boat,

If someone falls out,

Then they weren't meant to be in your boat anyway.

Dear Heart,

You are not alone

Everything you're going through is simply **happening** to you

It does not make you who you are.

It does not define you.

You can't accept your life where it is now as the final truth,

God has a plan for you.

Diamonds aren't made over night.

They're made by going through an immense amount of pressure.

Pearls aren't made overnight.

They're made by an oyster being uncomfortable, one unmoving grain of salt!

You are priceless, going through the fire to be purified.

Accept your purging, Beautiful, and you will find yourself in the King's jewelry box.

Dear Heart,

Just because you're broken doesn't mean you can't be fixed.

Each crack has a story

Each shattered line is a path to true love.

You just haven't met the right repairman.

Shambles don't define you

Artistry is in the eye of the beholder.

Someone will see the beauty in your flaws

Someone will take you and mold you into something magnificent.

It will be so beautiful that the cracks won't look like cracks anymore.

The cracks will piece together a delicate story.

Dear Heart,

In my quiet moments I think about:

How far I've come

How far you've come

How far we have to go

I think about our strengthens and our weaknesses.

The best that might happen

The worst that might come

And I am unafraid.

Dear Heart,

You'll find your soul mate soon enough.

You've made it this far.

You just keep pushing.

Just keep swimming.

Just keep beating.

Just keep thinking of the places we'll go.

Don't worry about perfection

We don't want the knight in shining armor,

That means he's never been in battle.

Dear Heart,

Being someone's first love is great,

But being their last love is beyond perfect.

I promise to keep working to be priceless,

I promise to treat you as the jewel you are.

Just like a diamond, I'll protect you.

Just like a ruby, I'll hide you in a safe

I'll give the key of the safe to he who deserves it.

Dear Heart,

You're young.

It feels like you've been through so much

But it hasn't been that long.

Everyone you let in won't hurt you.

The people who hurt you don't define the future loves.

Don't judge every person.

Hold tight to the light of love.

It will be unconditional and without blame.

It will be honest.

It won't seek to be callous or cause jealousy.

It will be kind

It won't hurt.

It will plant the seed of comfort deep in your spirit.

It will water the seed with grace and temperance

And love will grow.

One day.

Be patient.

Dear Heart,

I know you want a lot of things,

But I don't think you're ready.

Don't believe the hype of everyone else's possession.

You're not in a competition with anyone,

Obtaining things is a progression.

It appears that they have everything you want,

But there are always things unknown.

In the proper time, you will reap all the blessings from the love you've sown.

In His timing.

Dear Heart,

He left.

We already know this.

There's no need to dwell on it.

What _is_ worth dwelling on is what he taught you.

He taught you how to communicate,

He taught you what it was to share,

But most importantly he taught you how you wish to be loved,

You are worth waiting on,

You are a princess,

Waiting to be queened.

Dear Heart,

Don't let "I miss you" fool you.

Don't let, "I'm sorry" make you think about walking back

to something you know you don't need.

The longer you dance with the devil,

The longer you'll remain in hell.

Don't sell yourself short by settling.

You deserve more than what they can offer.

Remember, you left for a reason.

Remember the stress that caused you to leave.

Remember that you gave it your best,

That's all you could do.

Dear Heart,

Your attempt may fail,

But never fail to make an attempt.

Choose not to accept the false boundaries and limitations created by the past.

There are only three rules in life:

1. If you do not go after what you want, you'll never have it.
2. If you do not ask, the answer will always be no.
3. If you don't step forward, you will always be in the same place.

Break the glass ceilings of your own expectations in your life.

There is no finish line.

There is no ultimate goal.

You can always achieve more.

So dream big.

Dear Heart,

Worry is a waste of time.

It doesn't change a single thing in life.

All it does is steal your joy.

It keeps you from being focused on the most important

things in life.

Don't worry about a single thing.

If it's meant to be, it will.

If they're going to leave, they will.

If they can't accept you, escort them to the nearest exit.

You don't want enemies making camp here.

We only want conquerors.

We only want encouragers over here.

If they won't help you be a better version of yourself,

they weren't supposed to be there anyway.

Dear Heart,

Would you love yourself if you met yourself on the street?

If you wouldn't love you, how can you expect someone else to?

You are in no shape to give love, until you can properly receive it.

Receive it from yourself.

Give it to yourself.

Be your own teacher.

Then when you have effectively become student,

You may be the teacher.

Dear Heart,

Settle down!

Would you stop it!

I can't handle breathing and you fluttering.

It feels like birds are in my chest.

I already have butterflies in my stomach.

Maybe he could be the one.

I know you're wondering,

But let me think clearly...

Or else we'll end up losing...

Like last time.

Dear Heart,

I don't want to say "Told you so",

... So I won't!

You know what you did.

Always sticking love where it shouldn't be.

You're just too big!

From this moment on

YOU'RE IN TIMEOUT!

I don't care if you pout.

You're not willing to wait,

I have to dictate the wait.

Waiting takes more than a few months.

Love is time tested!

And God is the measure,

So stop!

I'll let you know when you can beat again.

Dear Heart,

Ouch.

I know you're hurting.

Life is unpredictable.

Don't fret!

Take heart little one.

They're angels now.

They're not gone forever,

Just for now.

You'll mend.

We don't break, just bend.

Dear Heart,

I know what you're thinking.

Don't take that tone with me.

I know he isn't the one.

But I'm lonely.

Settling isn't the way.

I know, I know!

Don't tell me what I should be doing.

You don't know what it's like

Always being lonely.

At least he's here now.

Ok, maybe you do know what loneliness is.

You don't know what it is to be a third wheel.

You don't know what it's like to plan your whole life only

for it to go completely off script.

You don't know what it's like when forever never comes.

You just know how I feel when I face my fears

So don't judge me.

Dear Heart,

You're a pearl,

At least you will be.

My body is the oyster.

These tribulations will take your grain of sand

And turn it into something beautiful.

Those exes will regret leaving.

Those friends will feel shame for their betrayals.

Everything is not always what it seems.

You will be too valuable in the future to believe your

current worth is dirt.

Their apology doesn't change what you deserve.

Dear Heart,

How is your love strong, but you weak?

You're going to hurt yourself.

You can't love those who intend to hurt you.

Love from a distance.

You can't love so hard without proper training.

Love God first!

Then your love will be herculean.

Dear Heart,

I saw a picture of him today.

I felt you wince.

I thought you weren't broken about him anymore.

He looked so happy.

It has been so long since we saw that smile.

Nice to know it still exists.

Sorry to know we couldn't keep it on his face.

It hurt to see him there.

He had no cares about the pieces he left behind.

Love would never be this unkind.

The memories of what we thought we had came flooding back.

And I realized we're not over him yet.

Dear Heart,

What, specifically, is God asking you to change today?
Imagine how good you will feel in a few months when you look back on all you have allowed God to accomplish in your life and through your grief.

I know it hurts right now, but it'll only hurt for a little while.

I promise lovecha after pain.

I promise flowers from small seeds.

Triumph in small dreams.

Dear Heart,

      I don't want a lukewarm love.

      I want it to burn my lips.

      I want it to engulf my soul.

      I want it to burn bridges of past lovers scorned

Dear Heart,

You are natural.

You are pure.

You are vibrant.

You are radiant.

You are everything God created you to be.

Everything you have gone through at this moment has made you into the person you are right now.

You are exactly who you should be.

You are everything you are supposed to be.

Enjoy it!

Relish in it!

Be you!

No one else!

Dear Heart,

It is not your job to keep him interested.

It shouldn't matter his hobbies.

His likes and dislikes will change.

It won't matter how he votes,

Or how often he goes to church.

His attractiveness at some point will fade,

That shouldn't be your focus.

Our focus is to flourish until he finds us.

He'll be interested because we're interesting.

He'll stay because he'll see the beauty in you.

He'll stay because he sees the value in you.

He'll stay because he marvels at the wonder of you.

And he'll stay because he's interested in everything about you.

Because you're worth someone's interest.

Not because you're trying to keep him interested.

Dear Heart,

A woman with a beautiful body is good for a night,

A woman with a beautiful mind is good for a lifetime;

But a woman with a beautiful heart is priceless.

I want to be good for everything.

I want to be good for life.

I want to be priceless.

I can't do that until you're good.

So be good!

Please?

Dear Heart,

Forgive him

Forgive her

Not for them

But for you

For me

For us

Unforgiveness is a poison.

It slowly chokes the life out of our dreams.

It kills the hope for greater goods.

It gives us more baggage then we can handle.

Forgive because we should.

Forgive because it does more for life than unforgiveness ever could.

Dear Heart,

When something disturbs the peace, you have to

LET IT GO.

The pain you have been through will only make you

stronger.

You must continue to love

Or you will wither away in sadness.

You don't have to be so untrusting

Not everyone is out to hurt you.

But you do have to be hesitant,

Not everyone knows how to love you.

Dear Heart,

They tell us we're so young,
No need to get committed and tied down.
But they don't understand.
They don't remember what it was like.
I try to tell them it just happens.
I try to tell them we're open to love, not looking for it.
There's never a "right time" to wait for it
So whenever the opportunity presents itself, take the risk.
Jump on the chance.

Dear Heart,
The time you spent waiting on them:
To change,
To apologize,
To recognize your worth
Could have been spent:
Achieving even more of your dreams,
Flying to higher heights,
Loving yourself that much more deeply,
And being happy.
Next time, don't waste your time.

Dear Heart,

Don't you dare dwell on the past.

Don't lounge in the things that could have been.

They weren't

They aren't

You are where you should be.

You are who you are and I love you for it.

Don't ever change!

Dear Heart,

Love says:

I've seen the ugly parts of you and I'm staying.

Lust says:

I've seen your beauty and I'm staying until it's gone.

Love says:

I value you.

Lust says:

I want you.

You choose who you want around.

Dear Heart,

When God closes a door,

Do not try to "pick" the lock.

Lay your expectations down.

Have your peace in walking away.

Take heart, dear heart, in trusting your Father,

He knows what you need.

He knows best!

If he says, "it needs to be closed,"

Don't get your fingers smashed by trying to keep the door open.

Dear Heart,

Be picky with whom you give your time to.

Be picky with how you spend your time.

It's ok to reserve your time, energy and intensity of spirit to those who reflect it earnestly.

Patience is always a virtue; an asset, an advantage.

Treat it as such.

Dear Heart,

There is no "one that got away."

The ones that left weren't meant to stay.

The ones that hesitated to go, weren't strong enough to stay.

The ones that seemed perfect, weren't as perfect as the one who will stay.

The one who will have the courage to stay,

Will never "get away,"

He'll find you as the best reason to stay.

Dear Heart,

You have to see the potential AND the "what is".
Don't get so caught up in what could be,
That you forget "what is".
Don't believe all the hype in "I will",
If you don't see any worth in "I am".
Sometimes it's ok to take the time to help others,
Other times, it only drags you down.
It's up to you to decide if you are tackling a project or the foundation of an empire.
That doesn't make you a gold digger either!
It makes you conscientious of your own empire.
It makes you a good steward of your time;
But most importantly it makes you aware of what you deserve.
We never settle.

Dear Heart,

I think you need some encouragement today.
I wanted to tell you that masterpieces aren't made over night.
All those mistakes and flaws are just sketches of who you used to be.
You can't appreciate or fully understand the greatness of a masterpiece,
Without seeing and appreciating the sketch it once was.
Don't get so focused on the doing and uninterested in the bigger picture.
If you don't respect, appreciate and acknowledge the journey,
You won't appreciate the destination.
It all has to be in perfect timing,
And unfortunately we don't get to watch the clock.
Take heart, my heart, all things are working together for His good,

In His perfect timing.

Dear Heart,

I'm not trying to be Cinderella.
I have entirely too many shoes anyway.
I don't want to be Belle,
I want a gentleman, not a beast.
I was never trying to be Tiana,
I know my life isn't up to magic or fate.
Prince Charming isn't my future,
The idea of him is fake.
My soul mate will be an imperfect person that tries every day of his life to love me unconditionally.
That in itself is hard to find, but that's the beauty in it.
I'm not looking.
He'll find me.
He'll find you.
Then he'll love you.
I'll pass along your message to him:
To my future husband,

My heart said:

I WILL WAIT FOR YOU

P.S. Come find us.

Dear Heart,

When someone tells you it can't be done,
(It's more a reflection of their limitations, not yours.)
Words are powerful.
These small things, full of letters, somehow cumulate to reflect how we feel and what we want.
Watch the words you speak, they generally become your actions, but most importantly,
Watch your actions.
These define who you will become.

Dear Heart,

Every adversity,

Every tribulation,

Every hard time, Every struggle

Is a seed of opportunity waiting to be a tale of victory.

Seize it.

Claim it

It shall reclaim all the failures you think you've had.

Soon, you will have conquered way more than what has ever conquered you

Dear Heart,

Do not apologize for wanting to be a wife and not a girlfriend.

Encourage your suitor to think of his vision and motives when approaching you

Don't lower your standards,

It's not becoming of a queen.

It demeans the crown.

Dear Heart,

Be kinder to your sister.

Be kinder to your brother

If you're not careful that

irritation will turn into anger,

anger will turn into bitterness.

You need not hate her for having excelled farther in life.

You don't know what God's measuring stick looks like.

Are you content with where you are in life?

No?

Then fix it.

No need to be focused on other people's things

when you have plenty of work to do

right where you are.

Dear Heart,
Do not be afraid to open yourself to others.
You'd be surprised at how much your pain resembles theirs.
Transparency is a luxury all cannot afford.
A fear just outside of many grasps.
I suggest you talk a little more.
Start the conversation,
So they can talk to their hearts as well.

Dear Heart,

Do you hear that knocking?

It's soft... but persistent.

Do you know who it is?

I know,

But He won't come in if you don't let Him.

He's too much of a gentleman to barge in.

It's our First Love,

Say yes to Him today.

Jesus Christ saves,

He knows the "him" He made just for you.

Just for me.

So invite Him in so He can tell us.

Here is a section to record the **conversation** you need to have with yourself. I hope you fill these pages and more.

Acknowledgments

First, I would like to give thanks to God and His Son Jesus Christ. I also want to acknowledge my supportive families; biologically, From the Heart Church Ministries, High Point University, friends and community. Special thanks to Mom, Karen Smith, Marshall Opie and LaBeverly Hooks for all of your edits and critiques of my book. Words could never express how appreciative I am for your time, sacrifice and believing in me, it means so much to me. To, all of my supporters, customers and readers, you hold a special place in my heart for allowing my dreams to come true. Also, I would like to give a special thanks to A. K Kpa for your assistance in the design of the cover page of this book. You always create and express the desire of my heart and bring my visions to life effortlessly.

Turn the page for a **preview** of "Surviving: Teenage Battlewounds"

Escape

Isolation, seclusion, loneliness, chilled to the bone
Find my refuge in feelings not shown
Small shelter, when the winds of life moan
I crawl between the letters within this page
Tears and cries buried under the happy girl on stage
Things no longer under her control to assuage
Periods, commas, all meaning much more
Each word containing life to restore
Watching the tide go in and out off shore
Release the dam of my soul
Pulling myself out of this self-dug hole

The First to Move
Brothers, sisters, black boys, and girls alike
It's time to give up the stereotypes
In ourselves we must fight
Fight hard and believe in each individual light
We must believe our value is worth more than
imagery
More valuable than the inches we have and
multimedia catastrophes
Something less complex than anatomy
And as important as this generational atrophy
Philosophy
So engrained it's become normalcy
And have we, seen no less than hypocrisy
The "greatest" make fashionable the ludicrous
But don't sag their pants, they wear straight cut tuxes
They don't speak text, money speaks suffix
And did educate mean only nerd and no friends
The idea of working eight hours seems to only offend
Simply working hard is something hard to come by
But hours invested into a job doesn't surpass the elite
Since when did the only money-making jobs become
rapper and athlete?
So you say, "We have no choice because we don't

sell clothes"
But the choice to wear pants two sizes too small was made on your own
It's ok, because everybody's doing it, yeah, it's what's in
What happened to creativity and being different
I like my battles to be the uphill kind
But I'm sick of being generalized

The world we live in is a product of our disguise
Choosing to be who we aren't is becoming our demise
I don't know any female who wants to be called ho
Or any male who wants to sell dope
If they do it's because they don't know better
We have to educate and stand together
It was only a century ago black meant beggar
Then, Black then meant educated
Now, Black can mean better
Don't be afraid to take possession of your purpose and your color
Color gives identity, color is the best of me

How do you know the sky?

Because it's blue

You know the grass by its color too

This is our time to change the meaning behind our names

Brown doesn't have to mean dirt; our brown black can mean land

Because we'll fight to take possession of what we own and deserve

From the example of our African heritage, we can take African American and preserve

That means care for, continue in, follow

It only takes one to lead…

So I'll go.

Future Generations Beware
What am I teaching my kids?

That it's ok to show my body?

And it's ok to lose my speech?

That our forefathers and mothers worked for equality

for null

That it's ok to lie and cheat?

That it's ok to let boys use me?

And allow men to forsake me, along with

commitment and love?

I don't want to teach them that but it's already out

there

So all I have to say is: Future generations beware.

What are you teaching your kids?

Are you leading them to favor black rappers over

black presidents?

Are you leading them to covet green dollars over

commitment?

Are you influencing them to talk down to women?

Or classify themselves with derogatory titles?

Is this sentiment the only direction for the future to

begin with despair?

If the above is the reasoning: Future Generations

Beware

What are we teaching our children?
That books fall useless to electronics?
Or that drinking and smoking is what accredits cool?
Are we encouraging escaping the ghetto?
Or are we accepting food stamps and welfare?
Please excuse my words if they seem harsh,
I'm just looking for some hope with these things I fear.
I don't want to be pessimistic but if there's hope tell me where
I have to be realistic. Future generations, beware.

Love Me For a Season
When the leaves are all but gone..

And the wind nips at your cheeks,

The fall has settled in..

And will only last few weeks.

Embrace and steal my warmth..

Hear my heart drop beats,

Know that it sings for you..

Every time our eyes should meet.

Love me..

When the sun kisses your skin...

Ocean waves toss to and fro,

We sit along the sand

And watch the stars begin to show.

Spending Summer in weather warm

My lady, take to my arm,

Cling to me so gently..

Know that these hands will bring no harm.

Love me.

Watching rain trickle down the glass..

Listening to spring's shower,
Washing away our troubles
If only for that hour.
The phones are disconnected
These moments only for us two,
You sleep against my chest..
In your dreams, I'll rescue you.

Love me.

When all is covered pure..
The white of winter day,
Snow lands along your hair..
For my fingers to brush away.
We kiss and laugh at mist..
We wrestle and you win,
Our love will never fade
And next year, we'll start again.

Love me.

To read more, purchase this book on jwerd.com

About the Author

Janae Werdlow graduated from High Point University with a B.S.B.A. in Entrepreneurship and owns a painting company. She has been writing since she was five years old. She was published twice in The Baltimore Review in 2009 and the American Library of Poetry in 2012.

Read more about her, her other books and how to contact her for speaking engagements at jwerd.com.

www.ingramcontent.com/pod-product-compliance
Lightning Source LLC
Chambersburg PA
CBHW070601170426
43201CB00012B/1890